Treats for your

CAT

HOW TO PAMPER YOUR PET:
PRACTICAL PROJECTS TO PROVE YOU CARE,
WITH OVER 400 PHOTOGRAPHS

PHOTOGRAPHY BY
JANE BURTON

LORENZ BOOKS

This edition is published by Lorenz Books
an imprint of Anness Publishing Ltd
Blaby Road, Wigston
Leicestershire LE18 4SE
info@anness.com

www.lorenzbooks.com
www.annesspublishing.com

If you like the images in this book and would
like to investigate using them for publishing,
promotions or advertising, please visit our website
www.practicalpictures.com for more information.

A CIP catalogue record for this book is available from the British Library.

Publisher: Joanna Lorenz
Senior Editor: Clare Nicholson
Consultant: Trevor Turner B.Vet. Med. M.R.C.V.S.
Special Photography: Jane Burton
Designers: Peter Butler and Susannah Good
Illustrator: Jane Molineaux
Production Controller: Mai-Ling Collyer

PUBLISHER'S NOTE
Although the advice and information in this
book are believed to be accurate and true at the
time of going to press, neither the authors nor
the publisher can accept any legal responsibility
or liability for any errors or omissions that may
have been made nor for any inaccuracies nor for
any loss, harm or injury that comes about from
following instructions or advice in this book.

CONTENTS

Introduction

This is a book for you and for the cat (or cats) you love. In it you will find hundreds of inspirations and ideas for ways to express your affection and devotion to the animal who occupies the central position in your life, and dozens of practical projects which will add to the quality of your cat's existence.

Discover how to make exquisite sleeping places and furnishings that will inject both style and elegance into your cat's life. Create unforgettable meals that will thrill your companion's taste buds: every cat is a gourmet at heart, and tempting treats are a sure way to strengthen the bond between you. Find out the games you can play with your cat, learn how to massage those feline tensions away, and on the spiritual side, uncover her mystic essence as revealed through awareness of the stars and their portents.

This is the ultimate manual for all caring cat owners, guaranteeing purry pets with bright eyes and bushy tails.

Cat Napping

op cats deserve the best, and battered baskets just won't do. Here's how to create cat castles and kitty carriers of their wildest dreams, whether it be a sea-cat box for a tom or an empire-style bed for a princess puss, along with the ultimate in interior trimmings, cushions, drapes and rugs – whether these are to lie in, scratch on or chew.

A life of luxury is what every cat desires above all. So indulge your cat's fantasies and create a home where she will feel happy to spend her day – cleaning or snoozing or watching the world go by.

Your cat will naturally want to spend a lot of time on your bed (whether or not you happen to be in it) if she feels that her own facilities are anything less than first class. So make sure the cat home you create is more luxurious and seductive than your own, so you both get a good night's sleep.

This empire-style boudoir bed is fit for the feline queen who rules your humble home. Draw the curtains when she needs a little peace and quiet.

No corner or container will be left unexplored when a little kitty is looking for somewhere to sleep.

Sitting Kitty

Statistically, your cat's principal hobby and "activity" will be snoozing, whether this is the full dream-filled sleep or the proverbial catnap. The amount of time and effort dedicated to this pursuit should be reflected in the elegance and suitability of the napping space. Here are a few inspired ideas for customized cat comfort and exquisite ambience. Either start from scratch or adapt your kitty's present resting place.

House your cats in style: like the rest of us they don't like to be restricted to snoozing in the bedroom alone.

Wicker is fine for a desirable residence, but as these two would testify, it needs to be carefully lined for comfort.

For a really special treat, provide a superb four-poster bed where your prince in exile can dream those regal dreams that come at the end of a hard day's ruling. The witty leopardskin motif is printed on fur-friendly synthetic material, of course.

Sea-cat Box

From catamaran to fleet fe-liner, any puss would love to be decked out like this sailor tom. Decorate an old fruit crate with paint and add a length of rope to provide essential easy access to a scratching post on long voyages.

You will need:

old box, such as a fruit crate • emulsion paints: blue, red and white • paintbrushes • PVA glue • long piece of rope • masking tape • toy wheels or old bottle tops • thin card • soft pencil • craft knife • stencil brush

3 Paint the toy wheels or bottle tops red and white, and leave to dry. Then to make a stencil of an anchor, draw an anchor on a piece of thin card. Carefully cut it out with a craft knife making sure you achieve a clear outline.

4 To decorate the box, paint red and white stripes along the front and glue on the wheels. Secure the stencil to the box with masking tape then apply white paint with a stencil brush – do not overload the brush with paint otherwise it may smudge. Remove the stencil and leave to dry.

1 Paint the inside and outside of the box with blue emulsion and leave to dry. Apply a second coat, if necessary.

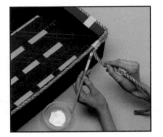

2 Glue the rope around the box, securing it with masking tape until it dries.

For extra tom cat comfort and style, pad the box with a calico cushion stencilled with anchors.

Transports of Delight

Travel broadens the mind but, while some cats adore being taken to new venues, others express extreme reluctance. Once there, of course, even the coolest of cats gains boundless pleasure from investigating the novel locale – to the extent that you may have trouble getting them home again. Every cat wants to travel in style, so don't settle for a standard "carrier unit": find or make something in which your companion can journey in luxury and comfort.

For carrying your cat in true style, hat boxes make excellent travel compartments – no sharp corners or jagged edges to disturb or inconvenience.

Picnic hampers can make ideal carry-baskets, but make sure you line the inside with some padded blanket or soft toning fabric. The aromas of old smoked salmon sandwiches and chicken breasts make for the perfect environment.

Jungle Carrier

If you want your cat to stand out in the urban jungle, paint your carrier to make it fit for a lion king.

1 Paint the basket white and allow to dry. With masking tape, mark out an hexagonal area on both sides of the carrier, then paint the rest of the basket blue. Allow to dry and apply a second coat, if necessary. Within the white areas paint lions' faces in yellow.

You will need:

cat carrier • emulsion paints: white, blue, yellow, red and black • paintbrushes • masking tape • varnish • varnishing brush

2 Then paint the rest of the hexagon red. This will be the mane.

3 When the paint is dry, add the facial features – eyes, nose, ears and mouth. Finally, to protect the carrier from the outdoor elements, paint it with a coat of clear varnish.

The ideal mode of transport for cats with a sense of adventure.

Leopard-look De Luxe Carrier

Fit for the boulevards of Paris, this high-style chic carrier is customized with fake fur fabric.

You will need:

flat-packed cardboard carrier • craft knife • pencil • paper for pattern • leopard-print fabric, enough to cover box • pins • needle and matching thread • double-sided tape • bias binding • band • gold buckle

1 Take the flattened carrier and cut a large rectangle at both ends of the carrier to create ventilation holes for the cat. (The existing holes will be covered by the material.) Then use the flattened carrier to make a paper pattern. You will need one pattern for both ends and one to cover the middle section. Draw the ventilation holes on your pattern. (See diagrams on page 92.)

Wild to be borne! Exotic, despotic and stylishly hypnotic, this sophisticated carrier will be well-spotted wherever you take it. Every trip will proudly remind your cat of the nobility of its ancestry.

2 Pin the patterns to the material and cut them out. Pin, tack and sew the two pieces of material which cover the inside and outside of each end, and the centre pieces. Cut a hole for the handle to slip through and the ventilation holes too.

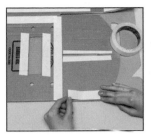

3 Before you cover the box, attach some strips of double-sided tape as shown, to secure the material. Turn the edges of material over and secure with double-sided tape. Assemble the box then fit the side pieces of material onto the carrier. Secure with double-sided tape.

4 To prevent the handles from fraying, stick double-sided tape onto bias-binding and attach to each edge. Fit the middle section of fabric over the rest of the carrier, sticking down any loose edges. Finally, embellish with a coloured band and a smart gold buckle.

Soft Furnishings

As everyone knows, cats are beings of infinite taste and discrimination – much more so, in most cases, than their owners. They take pride in their surroundings, and pleasure in their small luxuries. So, decorate your companion's space with meticulous attention to detail, try to furnish with flair and wit, and do keep your standards up to theirs.

Just as dogs dream of rabbits, so cats dream of fish. And what better way to encourage such delicious dreams than a fish-embroidered mat . . .

Tartan brings out the best in cats, especially tabbies. The rich colours enhance the glowing warmth of the coat (and the pattern hides any loose fur).

For country cats, sometimes a simple cushion in unassuming folk style suits best.

Sweet thoughts are ensured with this temptingly-embroidered blanket.

Compliment your cat with a personal portrait. The texture of tapestry can encourage a little creative work of their own, so protect the work from playful scratches with plastic mounting.

Pawprint Cushion

For festival days and special occasions, offer imperial-style comfort to your companion with this soft, luxurious velvet cushion. The stencilled pawprint pattern is specially designed to hide any muddy paw marks.

You will need:

tracing paper • soft pencil • thin card • craft knife • 0.5m (½yd) furnishing velvet • scissors • stencil brush • black fabric paint • pins • needle and matching thread • 1.75m (2yd) multi-coloured cord • four tassels • 40cm (16in) cushion pad

1 Trace the pawprint from the template on page 92. Transfer it onto the thin card. Repeat the template once more, leaving a wide margin all round.

The tassels provide a permanent toy on-site to help while away the hours.

2 Cut out the stencils with a craft knife.

3 Cut a 43cm (17in) square from the velvet and place on a flat surface. Stencil pawprints at random, to look as if a cat has walked over the cushion. Hold the brush upright, and hold the stencil firmly in place to avoid smudging. Leave to dry.

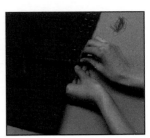

4 Make an envelope-style opening by cutting two 43 × 25cm (17 × 10in) pieces of velvet. Place each piece over the stencilled velvet, right sides together, so that they overlap in the middle. Turn over and finish off the edges that overlap. Pin and tack, then sew around the outside, leaving a 0.5cm (¼in) seam allowance. Turn right side out, trim with the cord and a tassel at each corner using stab stitch. Insert the cushion pad.

Feline Furniture

Although accessories like the cat flap and the litter tray may not at first inspire creative flair, there is no need for them to be grim and ghastly. In fact it is precisely these functional items that require most thought and attention. The litter tray is a very important part of your cat's life: it can cause embarrassment but it needn't if you surround it with a lovingly crafted privacy screen. Show how much you appreciate your cat and respect her dignity by paying attention to her quality of life at all levels.

A decorated doll's room becomes a perfect playpen for a little kitty.

Just to make sure no draughts disturb her, an exclusive excluder keeps your cat sitting pretty.

A delightful and discreet trompe l'oeil screen presents your companion decorously in front, while she completes her toilette behind.

First impressions are vital, so don't let the entrance to your cat's environment be a boring plastic rectangle. With a little ingenuity you can make it an attractive and welcoming feature.

Skyscraper Privacy Screen

This is the ideal way to hide your cat's litter tray from public view.

You will need:

four rectangles of mounting card: 50 × 40cm (20 × 16in), 55 × 10cm (21½ × 4in) and two 45 × 25cm (18 × 10in) • pencil • ruler • craft knife • four rectangles of MDF (dimensions as above) • paintbrushes • acrylic paints: black, terracotta, yellow and dark green • sponge • wood glue • upholstery tacks • four 2.5cm (1in) hinges

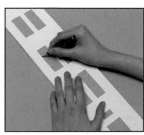

2 Take the mounting card and place it on top of its corresponding piece of MDF. Use it like a stencil to trace out the windows.

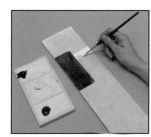

3 Decide which windows you want to look dark and paint them black, and paint the door area terracotta. Then paint the rest of the MDF yellow.

4 Sponge the terracotta paint onto the mounting card. Dilute the paint a little but not too much because if too wet it will warp the card. Decorate the three other pieces of board using the same technique and painting the front panel green and the sides terracotta.

1 Decorate each piece of mounting card in turn, starting with the tallest panel. Lightly draw the windows, door and cat's head onto the card. Cut them out with a craft knife.

New York, New York! Both you and your companion will be grateful for your consideration in making this cosmopolitan privacy screen.

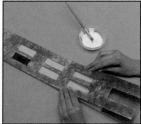

5 Glue all the pieces of mounting card onto their corresponding pieces of board. Glue the skyscraper onto the central panel. Add on any additional features. Then, decorate the top edges with upholstery tacks and paint the back dark green. Join the two sides to the central panel with hinges.

Finishing Touches

Your cat – and cats in general – are a very important part of your life, and you will want to embellish your home with images of your personal friend and other famous felines. You won't, of course, forget your cat's own interests while you go about this: make sure that some of your ornaments and hangings reflect your companion's passions – like a fun fish mirror before which she can clean and pose. With a little ingenuity there is hardly a decoration in your home that can't be pussonalized.

These lovely wooden ornaments could easily become toys if you don't keep a watchful eye.

Enhance a favourite feline photograph with a beautiful custom-made cat frame.

Birds on a line provide hours of amusement.

Wall decorations and plaques in cat-friendly motifs enhance any interior: the most popular designs in every catalogue are mice, fish . . . and cats.

Fish Reflections

Cats love gazing at their own reflection. So provide your companion with a deep-sea mirror.

You will need:

circular mirror • mounting card • pencil • craft knife • scissors • corrugated cardboard • PVA glue • masking tape • modelling clay • strips of newspaper • wallpaper paste • acrylic paints: light green, pale blue, red and black • paintbrushes • glass beads • double-sided tape

Contemplating their reflection is as much a source of fascination for cats as it is for us.

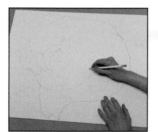

1 Draw around the mirror onto the mounting card. Draw a larger circle around this and use it as a guide to draw a basic fish shape. Cut out the outline – this will be the base – then a similar shape out of corrugated cardboard and glue it to the base. Cut several fins and scales from corrugated cardboard and build up a relief pattern.

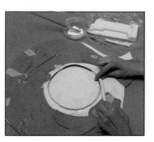

2 Cut a 1.25cm (½in) wide strip of card long enough to fit around the outside of the mirror. Glue this round the mirror and stick the strip down bit by bit using masking tape. Around this carefully place a strip of modelling clay.

3 Soak strips of newspaper in diluted wallpaper paste then start covering the corrugated cardboard. After the first layer is applied allow it to dry and then repeat the process several times.

4 Paint the fish with acrylic paints, highlighting the features and scales with fine black lines. Stick on glass beads to create the effect of water bubbles. Finally, place strong double-sided tape on the back of the mirror and stick in place.

On the Catwalk

Cats – males as much as females – are as "appearance-conscious" (ok, let's admit it, vain) as humans. Whereas most dogs are perfectly content to come home covered in mud and flop down to sleep, a cat wouldn't dream of being so sloppy. Your cat may spend hours each day ensuring perfect presentability, as every puss

wants to look her best at all hours of the day and night. Here are easy-sew projects for tailor-made, classic tartan winter coats or evening catsuits to kill for; along with daring accessories and high-style items such as the ultimate diamanté collar, the most stylish leash of the season, and a winter scarf. Assess the accessories and acquire the accoutrement – coats, collars, leads and other vital items – that will set free the catwalk model trapped in the heart of every fashionable feline.

Waiting on the podium to receive the gold medal for stylishness? Then wear this striking bright red halter encrusted with bold, daytime costume jewellery. This model presents paste with panache – and with a look that tells you in no uncertain terms that her real gems are locked in the safe back at the hotel!

Though more often associated with the dog world, leather and studs can be appropriated by the most delicate of felines to inject a hint of danger and machismo.

Overcats

Daytime strolls, a trip out in the car, a night out on the tiles – your cat leads a rich life and will require a proper variety of suitable attire. Outside, cat coats keep your cat warm in winter and cool in summer. Inside, they are just unashamedly fun, frivolous indulgences to flaunt and enjoy.

When there's a nip in the air, a light and airy jacket like this stencilled creation is just the ticket.

Sometimes, for those trips to town, a more sophisticated number is called for.

Tartan Tabby Coat

The basic pattern for this coat can be adapted to suit every need. Add fur trimmings for evening outfits or use waterproof material for outdoors.

You will need:

plain paper • pencil • scissors • 90cm × 115cm (1yd × 45in) tartan fabric • 90cm × 115cm (1yd × 45in) wadding • 90cm × 115cm (1yd × 45in) lining • safety pins • pins • needle and matching thread • bias binding • velcro fastenings • hook and eye

1 Scale up the template on page 93. Cut a square of the tartan large enough to take the pattern, then cut the wadding and the lining larger. Place the wadding on top of the lining then the tartan, and safety pin all the layers together.

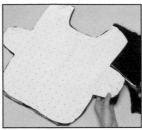

2 With the safety pins holding the three layers firmly, machine- or hand-quilt a rectangular pattern across the surface. Then remove the safety pins.

3 Lay the paper pattern on top of the quilted fabric, then pin and tack it in position. Carefully cut around the pattern.

4 If you want the coat to fit snugly, sew a small dart in the centre of the tail end of the pattern. Then remove the pattern.

5 Pin and sew the bias binding around the edge of the coat using slip stitch.

6 Sew velcro fastenings onto the flaps which will go under the chest.

7 To finish off, sew a hook and eye onto the neck opening of the coat.

The fuller cut on this outdoor cape is designed to protect during the severest winter. The perfect puss-suit for all pursuits.

Fancy Kit

When something more flamboyant is required, think Pussy Galore. There's no need to inhibit your imagination or your flair when assembling accessories for a suave, deliciously decadent affair. Ring the changes if your cat has a bit of Cat Woman or Top Cat inside (and what cat doesn't sometimes?), with a figure-hugging bodice or macho T-shirt.

If it's smart enough for your cat it will be smart enough for you, too – just make sure that you also have the grace and poise to carry it off. When you go to the effort of giving your companion the coat of her dreams, keep going and make a stylish match for yourself.

A feather boa can be lots of fun – and who knows, she might even end up wearing it!

For understated style and elegance, there's nothing to match the feel of pearls around her neck.

Reining your cat is a tricky issue – it impacts on dignity and can cause hurt pride. So, where your companion is headstrong and safety demands caution, soften the blow by providing a beautifully crafted harness that can be worn with panache.

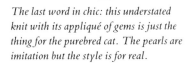

Of course, even the most aristocratic of cats occasionally wants to be a cool dude for a day. A trendy T-shirt is the ultimate in street style.

The last word in chic: this understated knit with its appliqué of gems is just the thing for the purebred cat. The pearls are imitation but the style is for real.

Enchanted Circles

Getting the main costume right is only a beginning: complementary detail is everything. Of course, if your cat decides to wear nothing more than its fur, then there's nothing but the detail to work with.

The first detail you *have* to get right is the collar. Consider personality, bearing, colouring, appearance, physical style and presence, before you develop your designs. Obviously your cat needs a wardrobe full of collars for every occasion – these are just a few ideas.

The perfect floral accessory for a picnic, christening, flower show, or any summer outdoor gathering. Why not embellish a straw hat for yourself with matching flowers?

3 Fold the picot-edged ribbon in half, and with matching cotton slip stitch the underside down to cover the raw ends of the ribbon on the back. Sew the buckle catch onto one end of the ribbon.

Catmaiden Collar

For a summer wedding, nothing is prettier than a floral decoration.

You will need:

silk flowers in three different colours • 30cm × 1.25cm (12in × ½in) purple picot-edged ribbon • needle and matching thread • small glass beads • 20 × 0.5cm (8 × ¼in) satin ribbon in gold and in green • 1.25cm (½in) gilt buckle and catch • 7.5cm (3in) small piece of elastic • bell

1 Remove the individual flowers from the main stalk and take out the plastic stamens. Starting 5cm (2in) from one end, sew them firmly onto the picot-edged ribbon, alternating the colours. Stitch a bead into the centre of each flower. Cover about 15cm (6in) of the ribbon in this way.

2 Cut 5cm (2ih) lengths from the gold and green satin ribbons and sew them onto the back of the picot-edged ribbon at intervals, twisting them into loops. Fold the stamens in half and stitch onto the ribbon in groups of two or three to fill any gaps.

4 Fix the buckle onto the elastic. Trim the loose ends of ribbon to length, so that the collar will fit the cat comfortably, then turn the raw edges under. Stab stitch the elastic between them, stitching firmly. Finish off by attaching a bell.

Jewelled Collar

Flair is simple to add: take a basic collar and embellish with jewels to transform it for a special occasion.

You will need:

double-sided tape • 20 × 5cm (8 × 2in) black velvet ribbon • sew-on jewels in pinks and purples • needle and matching thread • small gilt buckle • 15 × 2.5cm (6 × 1in) red velvet ribbon

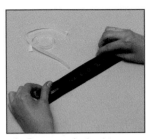

1 Remove the backing from one side of the double-sided tape and stick it along the centre of the wrong side of the black ribbon. Peel off the second backing paper and fold one of the long sides of the ribbon over the length of the tape.

Ready for romance or romping: an all-purpose fun collar ideal for anything from a candlelit supper with someone special (maybe even you!) to a night on the town with the girls.

2 Sew on the jewels firmly along the folded edge, using a double length of thread, and arranging the colours alternately to form an interesting pattern.

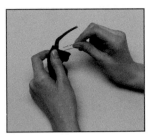

3 Neaten the raw edges, then make a small loop at one end to enclose the buckle. Stitch in place. Make a fastening tab from the folded red ribbon at the other end.

4 To finish off, fold over the loose side of the black velvet and stitch in place.

This junior collar handcrafted in cheerful buttons is the ideal first fashion statement for the young at heart.

Vital Accessories

High fashion – especially for cats – is above all a joyously irreverant celebration of the unnecessary – which is why it is so enormously satisfying.

Slippers may have some small function for slouching around the house, or chewing on, but of course they should also look cool and sophisticated should visitors chance to call. Ribbons and bow ties are a frivolous delight, and you can expect a lot of hilarity as you attempt to tie them on. An elegant bow tie transforms any toe-tied tabby into Fred Astaire, while the touch of decadence created by a ribbon turns the shyest kitten into his Ginger Rogers.

Pastel-coloured pussy boots for trips to town

The simplest, and in many ways most elegant accessory, is a sleek satin ribbon.

A daisy-chain collar won't last longer than an afternoon, but will be a source of pride for both of you.

A comfortable scarf, casually worn, will impress friends and unexpected callers.

Bow Tie

Any suave cat will need a range of these simple-to-make bow ties in different colours: from stylish black for formal wear, to bold tones and patterns for parties and celebrations.

You will need:

30 × 30cm (12 × 12in) white cotton fabric • embroidery hoop • soft pencil • gold outliner pen • fabric pens in a variety of colours • scissors • 20 × 20cm (8 × 8in) red cotton fabric • pins • needle and matching thread • velcro • cat collar

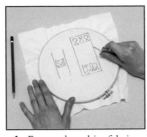

1 Fasten the white fabric into the hoop. Using a soft pencil, mark out a rectangle 14 × 7.5cm (5½ × 3in) for the bow and another 10 × 4cm (4 × 1½in) for the central band. Leave room for seam allowances between the rectangles. Draw patterns on both rectangles then paint over with the gold outliner pen and leave to dry.

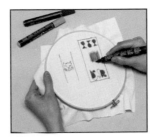

2 Using the fabric pens, fill in the shapes. Colour in the rectangles and a 1.5cm (½in) seam allowance all around. Cut out the rectangles, including the seam allowance. Then cut two rectangles from the red fabric to the same size.

3 Fold the edges under 1.5cm (½in) to the wrong sides on both the painted rectangles and the red ones. Place the two rectangles for the bow together, wrong sides facing, and pin. Tack then sew them together. Repeat for the central band.

4 Sew two rows of gathering threads along the centre of the bow. Gather to make it approximately 2.5cm (1in) deep. Machine- or hand-sew the central band to the front of the gathered bow tie.

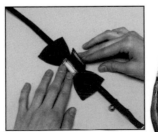

5 Finally, sew strips of velcro to the central band at either end. To finish fasten to a cat's collar.

This sophisticated beau will dance tonight away with you in London, and buy you breakfast in Paris tomorrow morning.

Gourmet Catering

The way to every pet's heart is through its stomach. Kitty's senses of taste and scent are far more developed than our own, so it seems quite unfair to bore her with mass-produced fare. Start hunting for catnip and fish oil, and stock up on anchovies and sardines . . . these delectable recipes guarantee happier, healthier pets. From feline fish fancies to mackerel TV munchies, this is the food your four-legged friend will favour.

Although the easiest way to ensure your cat enjoys a balanced diet is to feed her daily on canned cat food thoroughly mixed with a handful of fibre, once or twice a week serve up some kitty cuisine to add interest to the diet. Your cat will love the taste and texture of "real" food and appreciate the change: and you will enjoy giving her a tasty treat.

This stunning table centre is also the guest of honour! Like the rest of us, cats can sense, and love, a sophisticated setting, and any meal can be made an event with special touches such as these.

The treats in this chapter will certainly tip the scales. By all means pamper your pet with these gourmet delights and special delicacies – but do watch your companion's weight, as over-eating or any tendency to fat can be very unhealthy.

TV Snacks and Titbits

When you're curled up in an armchair with your favourite snack and your fantasy movie star, don't forget your real loved one! Put together a selection of these feline foodstuffs and your cat will be right there snuggled up with you. Unless otherwise indicated, all recipes make one serving for one adult cat.

Eggstacy

15ml/1 tbsp olive oil
1 egg
30ml/2 tbsp milk
25g/1oz grated cheese

Put the oil in a small frying pan and place over a low heat. Beat the egg and milk together. Once the oil looks medium-hot, slowly pour in the mixture, then gently coddle with a wooden spoon, ensuring the mixture doesn't start to fry. Add the grated cheese to the centre of the mixture, and fold over the edges when firm. Cook until quite stiff, cool, then cut into bite-sized pieces.

Sardine Soup is a fishy favourite

Sardine Soup

2 tinned sardines
knob of butter
250ml/8fl oz water
few stalks of watercress
fish sauce (optional)

Put the sardines and the knob of butter into a heavy-based frying-pan and place on a medium heat. As the pan warms and the butter melts, mash the sardines into it. When the butter has completely melted, pour in the water and stir as it comes to the boil. Thoroughly shred the watercress and toss into the pan. Remove the pan from the heat and allow to cool. Liquidize, and add a dash of fish sauce.

The perfect brunch for those lying-in days

Mouseburger Bites

75g/3oz sausagemeat or finely
minced beef
30ml/2 tbsp oatmeal
1 egg, to bind
whisker of catnip, finely chopped

Knead the ingredients together very
thoroughly and form into a flat oval.
Grill under a medium heat for 5–7
minutes, turning frequently, until the
outside is crisp. Wait until cool, then
slice into bite-sized chunks.

Cheese delights for cat dreams

*Sneaking downstairs for a midnight feast
is not only the perogative of small
children . . .*

Burger bliss for TV snacks

Cheese *Please!*

50g/2oz grated cheese
25g/1oz plain yogurt or soured cream
a little oatmeal
25g/1oz margarine or low-fat spread

Mash all the ingredients together,
adding them in the order indicated
above, and serve cold. No cooking is
required for this dish. Some cats will
not take to this dish as it is not
meat-based: others will love it.

CAT'S TIP
*For a really quick gourmet treat, buy
your cat a small package of luxury cat
food and dice it up while it is still in its
container – this is much more interesting
than if you put it on a plate or in a bowl.*

just a quick nibble, nothing more . . .

Fish Fantasies

It is extremely rare to find a cat that doesn't adore seafood, yet often, having spent a lifetime eating the canned variety, they will be confused if you put raw fish in their bowl. Cooked fish is another matter and you will see her excited reaction when you start to prepare it. These fishy treats are certain to delight your companion.

When it comes to finishing a tasty meal, a truly satisfied puss will sit and wash its face with its paw.

Nutrition

So far as useful nutritional content per gram or ounce is concerned, fresh salmon is excellent, but fresh or canned sardines come close behind and are preferred by many if not most cats. Canned kippers, tuna or smoked mackerel are other good options.

If serving canned fish of any kind, it is a good idea to mash in some fibre in the form of oatmeal or cooked barley. With all fish dishes, make sure there is plenty of drinking water available in a separate bowl.

Canned pilchards

Heads and tails

Sliced kipper in cream

Tasty trout treats

Crispy Trout Pieces

Serves Two

1 egg yolk
1 small trout fillet
45ml/3 tbsp oatmeal
15ml/1 tbsp vegetable oil

Preheat the oven to 180°C/350°F/Gas 4. Beat the egg, dip the fish in it, and then coat it with oatmeal. Put the oil in a small baking pan and lay the fillet in it, turning it over once or twice. Bake for 15 minutes, turn over, and bake for 15 minutes more. Remove the fish to a dish, allow to cool, and cut into bite-sized pieces.

Serving suggestion: if it looks a little dry, add a dash of cream.

Mackerel Magic

Serves Two

*1 medium-sized rasher unsmoked bacon,
rind removed, grilled
75g/3oz cooked brown rice
10ml/2 tsp soy sauce, mushroom soy
sauce or mushroom ketchup
1 fresh mackerel, headed, tailed, cleaned
and scaled*

Chop the bacon up small and mix
with the rice, adding the sauce in
dashes as you go. Grill the mackerel
on both sides until crispy brown.
Allow to cool, then split it along the
stomach and gently open it out.
Bone, working from head to tail. Fill
with the rice and bacon mixture,
close over the sides of the mackerel.
and serve.

Fish heaven for good cats

Kipper Suprême

Serves Two

*100g/4oz cooked kipper
75g/3oz leftover cooked root vegetables
2 eggs
a little milk
50g/2oz grated cheese*

Preheat the oven to 160°C/325°F/
Gas 3. Mash together the fish and
vegetables. Put the mixture into an
oiled baking tin. Beat the eggs, milk
and cheese together, and pour on top
of the fish mixture. Bake for about 20
minutes, until the outside is firm but
the inside is reasonably soft. Remove
from the oven and allow to cool.

CAT'S TIP
*Cats love plain smoked fish, but it is very
salty and too much is not good for them.
Whenever you eat it let your cat have just
the skins and tails.*

Kedgeree

*50g/2oz white rice
½ pickling onion, peeled and finely
chopped
15g/½oz margarine or low-fat spread
75g/3oz cooked kipper or smoked
mackerel, skinned and boned
½ hard-boiled egg, shelled and finely
chopped
yolk of 1 egg
7.5ml/½ tbsp pouring cream*

Cook and drain the rice. While the
rice is cooking, gently fry the
chopped onion in the margarine until
soft. Add the fish and the egg and
continue cooking, stirring all the
time with a wooden spoon. Mix in
the rice, still over the heat, and stir
until everything seems steamy hot.
Blend in the egg yolk, then the
cream. After a last few stirs, tip onto
a plate and leave to cool.

A fish in a dish

Catty Kedgeree

Chicken Choices and Meat Treats

In general, poultry dishes are less calorific than meat recipes: gram for gram and ounce for ounce, breast of roast chicken has little more than half the calories of a lightly fried beefburger. So, if your cat has a tendency to put on weight (not that you would ever comment, of course), serve poultry in preference – and try also to include vegetables and fibre, in the form of bran from health food shops, which have low calorific value. Always check cooked poultry very carefully for bones – these can be dangerous.

Lean, keen and ready to preen. As all this lip-smacking confirms, plenty of chicken is essential in the diet of any health-conscious cat. It's an ingredient on which they can comfortably fill up on without filling out.

Chicken Cheeseburger

Serves Two

50g/2oz finely minced beef
50g/2oz finely minced chicken
15ml/1 tbsp canned thick chicken soup
50g/2oz wholegrain breadcrumbs or oatmeal
1 baby carrot, cooked until soft
1 egg
25–50g/1–2oz grated cheese

Mash the meat and chicken with the soup, then add the breadcrumbs or oatmeal, mushy carrot and egg. Make into two small burgers and grill (leaving much rarer than you would for yourself). Sprinkle with grated cheese and grill again until the cheese is melted. Allow to cool until warm to the touch, and serve. (Why not grill one of the burgers for longer and eat it yourself? That way you can genuinely share a meal with your companion.)

Mince magic for cats

Surf "n" turf, cat-style

Chicken with a Sardine Crust

Serves Two

1 can sardines in olive oil
50g/2oz wholegrain breadcrumbs
1 egg, beaten
2.5ml/½ tsp brewer's yeast
2 cooked chicken drumsticks,
bones removed

Drain the sardines, reserving the olive oil, and mash. Mix in the breadcrumbs, egg and yeast to an even, gooey consistency. Coat the chicken drumsticks evenly in the mixture. Heat the reserved olive oil in a frying pan, then add the coated drumsticks and fry, turning frequently, until brown. Remove from the heat, and cool before serving.

Rabbit Chasseur

Serves Two

3–4 canned prunes, stoned
15ml/1 tbsp vegetable or olive oil
75g/3oz rabbit, cut into 0.5cm
(¼in) cubes
15g/½oz flour
15ml/1 tbsp tomato juice
1–2 pinches of chopped catnip
15ml/1 tbsp canned thick chicken soup

Mash the prunes coarsely on a plate, then heat the oil in a frying pan and add the diced pieces of rabbit, frying them until they are pale brown. Add the mashed prunes, stir and sprinkle in the flour and stir. Continue frying until the coated pieces are a golden brown. Remove the pan from the heat and immediately add the tomato juice, catnip and soup, continuing to stir gently for a further 2–3 minutes. Remove the food from the pan to a separate dish and allow to cool before serving.

Run rabbit, run rabbit...

Truly meaty morsels

Organ Duet

1 chicken liver, finely chopped
½ lamb's kidney, finely chopped
1 small rasher unsmoked bacon, rind
removed and finely chopped
1 baby carrot, cooked
15ml/1 tbsp wholegrain breadcrumbs
or oatmeal

Put the meat into boiling water for 3 minutes. Drain off the water, then blend the meat with the carrot and breadcrumbs or oatmeal for a few seconds (leave some texture), or mash the mixture together with a fork. Cool until warm to the touch.

CAT'S TIP
To add an extra treat, serve a dish of catnip tea. Simply pour boiling water onto shredded catnip leaves (15–20ml/ 3–4 tsp catnip per 600ml/1 pint). Once cool, cover, and keep in the fridge.

Entertaining with Ease

Always feed your cat before inviting her friends round: unless she is unusually well-adjusted, she is likely to resent the intrusion of other cats into "home territory", no matter how friendly she might be under different circumstances. Feeding in advance will lower the tension and put everyone at their ease. Then it is a good idea to keep back a little treat for her – something as simple as a bowl of milk – as a symbol of her proprietary rights. The guests should be served on "neutral" plates – not your companion's regular bowls and dishes.

Etikit

Give each cat a separate dish, and serve everyone at once, or at least in quick succession. Once a cat is comfortable with its own plate, squabbles are unlikely so long as the portions are equal and everyone has enough to eat.

If the cats are old friends and are used to eating together, you can risk serving the banquet for the entire company in a single dish. There will inevitably be some jostling, but usually it will be fairly good-natured.

Entertaining can be a nerve-racking experience for kittens, so let them get used to it gradually and make allowances for lapses in table manners.

It is never too early to teach the basics of floor etiquette. These two kittens have learnt the art of politely taking turns, and will enjoy social gatherings much more in consequence.

Party time for fruity cats

Fruit Cocktail

2 tsp melon, cut up fine
2 tsp white grapes (seedless),
cut up fine
2 tsp kiwi fruit, cut up fine
1 segment satsuma, cut up fine
1–2 tbsp plain yogurt, pouring cream
or cottage cheese

Mix up the fruit together, pour on the yogurt, cream or cottage cheese and fold in. Serve chilled.

Salmon Mousse

100g/4oz cooked salmon, skin and
bones removed
125ml/4fl oz skimmed milk
25g/1oz margarine, softened or
low-fat spread, creamed
1 drop cochineal food colouring
several cooked, shelled prawns
up to 125ml/4fl oz aspic jelly

This party dish always impresses.
The quantities serve three or four as a
main course – or twice that many as a
starter.

Mash the cooked salmon and
gradually add the milk; alternatively,
put the cooked salmon and the milk
in a blender or food processor and
process until creamy. Stir in the
margarine or low-fat spread, add the
cochineal, and beat vigorously until
stiff. Put in a glass bowl or a mould
so that the mixture fills it by three-
quarters. Chill for 20 minutes, then
decorate with the cooked prawns,
and pour on just enough heated aspic
to cover them. Once this layer has
set, add further aspic to taste and
leave for an hour or two in a cool
place or the fridge. To serve, turn the
mousse out onto a plate and divide
into portions.

Fishy treats

Sensational salmon

Fabulous Fishballs

Serves Eight

3 baby carrots, cooked until soft
200–400g/8–16oz canned tuna in
olive oil, drained
50g/2oz cooked kipper, skin removed
30ml/2 tbsp wholegrain breadcrumbs
or oatmeal
30–45ml/2–3 tbsp grated cheese
10ml/2 tsp brewer's yeast
several pinches chopped catnip
1 egg, beaten
30ml/2 tbsp tomato purée (not ketchup)

Preheat the oven to 180°C/350°F/
Gas 4. Mash the carrots with the fish,
breadcrumbs or oatmeal, cheese,
brewer's yeast, catnip, egg and
tomato purée to an even paste.
Mould into small balls and put on a
greased baking tray. Bake for 15–20
minutes, checking frequently: the
fishballs should be coloured and feel
firm. Cool thoroughly.

Special Occasions

Its important to bring your pet into family festivities like Christmas, birthdays, Easter and Hallowe'en. You might find that (rather like humans) they will feign indifference at first, but more usually they will become tremendously excited and get into everything, making a fearful nuisance of themselves.

Birthday Suggestion: Celebrity Fishcakes

As a little extra to be offered on this most special occasion, take a commercial frozen fishcake and thaw it out. Mash it and shape it into your cat's favourite fantasy – a mouse, a fish, or even a significant other cat.

Commercial fishcakes have already been cooked, so you can serve this dish cold, or bake it for 10 minutes in a medium oven (180°C/350°F/Gas 4), then cool.

Shaped to perfection

Valentine's Day

If you can bear to serve your companion a bad pun on Valentine's Day, do remember that cat's *love* heart.

More in harmony with the spirit of the occasion would be heart-shaped morsels: most of the "burger" and baked recipes in this book can be moulded in this way. Or pipe heart motifs on any favourite dish – use mashed potato on hot food or cream on cold.

My heart belongs to you

All My Heart

¼ green or red pepper, diced
7.5ml/½ tbsp olive oil
50g/2oz beef heart, very finely diced
25g/1oz grated cheese

Fry the pepper for a couple of minutes in the olive oil. Add the heart and keep frying until it starts to brown. Put everything in a bowl and, while it is still hot, mash in the cheese. Cool and serve.

Easter

Around Easter, you should be able to find egg moulds. These make the perfect special occasion serving dish for Easter.

Easter Scramble

5ml/1 tsp butter, margarine or
low-fat spread
2 medium-sized eggs
120ml/4 fl oz skimmed milk
chopped catnip to taste

In a small saucepan melt the butter or fat slowly over a very low heat. Beat the eggs, milk and catnip together, pour into the pan, and stir vigorously. Keep stirring, more gently, until the mixture scrambles, then remove from the pan, and cool. Tip the scramble into an egg mould and serve. (It's probably wise not to give your cat any further egg-based dishes for a few days.)

Cat eggstravaganzas

Hallowe'en

Buy a small swede or turnip and hollow it out. Carve the front with eyes, nose and mouth, but not right through: leave a thin membrane of flesh between the internal hollow and the carved features. Put a candle or nightlight inside, light it and the features should glow spookily. Your cat will find this a fascinating object, but don't push her too close, and don't allow the candle to burn too long. When your cat gets bored with the toy, leave it to cool, remove the candle and pour in a tasty mixture that she will love to scoop out, such as cod's roe.

The wild spirit within your cat comes into its own at Hallowe'en . . .

Something fishy

Roe Dip

*1 tomato, peeled and
very finely chopped
5ml/1 tsp olive oil
100g/4oz canned or pressed unsmoked
cod roe
20ml/1 generous tbsp pouring cream*

Fry the tomato in the oil until soft then remove from the pan. Crumble the roe, and mash in the cream and then the tomato, either in a blender or by hand, until you have a smooth creamy texture. Chill in the fridge, then scoop generously into the Hallowe'en mask or turn into a mould for a birthday dish.

Christmas and Thanksgiving

Naturally your cat will be an essential guest, so roast a personal poussin before you start roasting the turkey for the rest of the family. Let your cat savour the aroma of the bird while hot, but no picking at this stage, as the small bones can be dangerous. Cool the poussin in the fridge while you're roasting the turkey; then bone it, carve the meat, and serve with seasonal garnishes.

Puss poussin

*CAT'S TIP
Do note that while cats can cope with raw egg yolks, uncooked whites are extremely bad for them, as they contain an enzyme that breaks down biotin, a vitamin your cat needs: never serve your cat raw egg white in any shape or form.*

Designer Dishes and Customized Catlery

Dishes decorated in appropriate motifs can bring a little extra magic to supper time – as can cat mats and all the other accessories and atmospheric additions that go to enhance the perfect dining environment.

If you decorate your dishes with cats such as these then carry the theme through to the rest of the table accessories.

Putting the finishing touches to the table setting before the guests arrive.

Mice and Cheese Plates

If you are lucky, you may come across tableware that is already decorated with your cat's favourite motifs. Otherwise, it is easy to make your own designs – painted freehand, stencilled or stamped. Use paints that are non toxic, as the dishes may come in for a good licking.

It doesn't take long – or require any previous artistic training or great skill – to paint the bowls and plates you use for your cat's meals.

You will need:

plain white ceramic plate • black, non toxic, water-based craft enamel (for use on ceramics) • fine paintbrush

1 Clean and dry the plate thoroughly. Using the black enamel, paint the mice around the edge of the plate. When dry, paint the mouse in the centre, making long, thin, tapering strokes for the whiskers. Place the plate into a cold domestic oven and bake for 30–45 minutes at 160°C/ 325°F/Gas 3. Do not remove until it has cooled.

Pussy Place Mat

This simple place mat will help keep the floor around kitty's food bowl nice and clean. Make sure that the central fish motif is slightly larger than your cat's bowl so that the head and tail poke out from under the bowl.

You will need:

coloured felts • scissors • fabric glue • clear plastic • paintbrush • needle and thread

1 Cut out the basic shapes from felt. You will need a larger square; two oval shapes, one slightly larger than the other; a smaller oval shape; a fish shape; several small white circles; and four small stars.

2 Assemble the design as shown in the picture, then carefully glue the pieces in place.

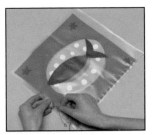

3 To protect the mat, trap the felt between two pieces of clear plastic. Sew around the edge with running stitch. Cut away any excess plastic.

Charming, simple and transforms a snack into a feast – a gift that will be appreciated and used time and again.

Glamour Puss

E very pusscat likes to look good on the tiles, and time spent in the bathroom and boudoir is an essential part of the daily regime. This chapter provides invaluable advice on how to create the appropriate setting, with full techniques for perfect puss presentation and beauty care treatments.

All cats need to be pampered, and the ultimate wash-and-brush-up guide gives grooming techniques, massage and aromatherapy tips, home beauty-parlour treatments and decorative fur stylings.

Your cat is already beautiful to you – but she also needs to feel consistently good about herself. This is how to go about it.

Cleaning and grooming make for a healthier, happier cat: inner contentment and well-being will follow naturally from external trimness, glossiness and feline elegance.

A personal vanity case for special cat care accessories is an essential part of the wardrobe.

Bathed in Splendor

This is not a question of hygiene: most cats are so scrupulous in their habits and personal cleanliness that they never actually need a bath at all. What is under discussion here is *pampering* – the indulging in the sybaritic pleasures of the bath. Although cats don't enjoy the sensation of luxuriating in scented waters like the rest of us, if you accompany the bathing with lots of stroking, petting and massaging, it will ensure complete cat heaven.

Bathed, powdered and perfumed – all dressed up and ready to go.

Introduce your kittens to the concept of bathing and grooming at an early age.

If you have two cats, they may take the task of beauty care into their own hands with mutual grooming techniques.

Bathtime Accessories
A couple of cotton wool balls
A shower attachment
Cat shampoo (don't use regular human shampoos)
A good cat comb or brush
A portable hair-dryer
Soft, scented towels

Bathtime

For the ultimate bathtime experience, flickering candles and subdued music will set the mood.

You will need:

washing bowl and pitcher • cat shampoo • natural sponge • several large towels • brush and comb

Of course, with few exceptions, cats are instinctively clean: any cat will groom itself far better than you could hope to. Your cat's first step is to lick clean the paws; then to use tongue and paws to clean every inch of the body.

1 Fill a bowl half full with warm water. Test the temperature, then lift the cat into the bowl and hold firmly. Wash with warm water, making sure the fur is really wet, then apply the shampoo, following the manufacturer's instructions. Massage the shampoo into the cat's coat but do not get shampoo in her eyes.

2 Rinse the cat with warm water, making sure that all the shampoo is out of her coat. Then take several large, warm, soft towels and gently rub dry.

3 Finally, start a long and luxurious session of gentle combing, making sure that you get out all of the snarls. For speed you can use a hair-dryer but your cat may not approve.

Good Grooming

Cats adore being groomed: the combination of stroking, attention and tidying makes them purr euphorically. When your companion gets the habit you will need to spend more and more time keeping her happy – not something that is likely to be a problem for you!

Start the grooming session with a period of preliminary caressing with the fingers. Stand your cat facing away from you and softly stroke all over her body, gently massaging the skin and feeling the fur for any dirt or matted areas. You will then be ready to proceed to the more advanced techniques described on these pages.

A rubber brush is ideal for massaging your cat. Work with circular movements and she is sure to help you by manoeuvring as you go.

Grooming a Short-haired Cat

Short-haired cats need very little grooming as they are very adept at keeping themselves clean. However, they certainly won't say no to a little extra help, particularly if you incorporate a little massage into the routine.

You will need:

metal comb • rubber brush • coat conditioner • soft cloth

3 Continue combing from head to tail.

1 Introduce your cat to the tools of the trade.

4 Use the rubber brush to remove any loose hair, and apply a few drops of coat conditioner.

2 Start by grooming with the metal comb, working down the sides.

5 Finish off by using the cloth to shine the coat.

Grooming a Long-haired Cat

Grooming has two objectives: a beautifully turned out companion; and a relaxed, good-natured friend.

You will need:

*wide-toothed comb •
rubber brush*

1 Start by combing out all the difficult knots and tangles in the coat.

2 Work your way down the sides and then under the chest.

3 Don't forget the tail. Make sure you gently comb out all of the knots.

4 You may need to sort out some of the tangles with your hands.

5 To get out some of the loose hair, comb your cat's fur upwards.

6 Use a rubber brush to get out old fur. Work with circular movements.

7 Soon your cat will be treating this as a game.

Whether short-haired or long-haired, you need a mirror to admire the results.

All primed for first prize in the cat show . . . and ready to have another go with the comb.

Vanity Accessories

The number of different grooming and beauty tools a cat requires is not huge – but over time, as with any much-loved hobby, you will accumulate dozens of perfect little items, including a special gadget for each small task. Any good pet shop will be able to supply you with the basics; after that, use your skills as a collector and artist to find and fashion your own customized range.

Remember, grooming time should be fun for both of you, and will be even more appreciated if everything looks enchanting.

Fancy Brush

Even the most dignified of long-haired cats can get into a tangle just through the most innocent romp. Making this decorative brush will persuade them to endure the indignity of tidying themselves up.

1 Sand the brush to remove any varnish, smooth down the surface, then paint gold. Leave to dry and apply a second coat if necessary.

You will need:

small, soft-bristled wooden brush • sandpaper • gold acrylic paint • paintbrush • silver doily • scissors • PVA glue • diamantés in various colours • matt craft varnish • varnishing brush

2 To decorate the brush, select small, interesting motifs from the paper doily and cut out neatly. Stick down with PVA glue.

3 Embellish the brush by adding diamantés and coat with a layer of matt craft varnish (avoiding the jewels) to protect the cut outs.

Vanity Case

All of your cat's vanity accessories can go into this elegant case, to be brought out whenever it's time for a grooming session.

You will need:

pink silk or satin lining • scissors • hat box • double-sided tape • thin card • small amount of wadding • glue • paintbrush • tiger-print fabric • handbag mirror • needle and matching thread • gold tassel • pencil • 0.5m (½yd) gold cord

2 Glue the fur-covered circle to the top of the lid. Then cut a smaller disc out of card to fit inside the lid and cover with lining fabric. Fix the mirror to the centre with double-sided tape. Secure the disc inside the lid using double-sided tape.

Perfect for home or travels abroad – try to choose a shade of fake fur that does not clash with your cat.

3 Sew the tassel onto the centre top of the lid.

5 Line the inside of the box with pink fabric. Cut a disc of card slightly smaller than the base and cover it too. Stick in place so that it covers the raw edges of the lining in the box.

4 Put the lid onto the box, then draw round the rim. Using this guideline as the top edge, cover the main box with fur fabric. Pierce a hole halfway down each side and thread the cord to form a carrying handle.

1 Cut a strip of pink fabric to cover the inside and outside of the rim of the box lid, allowing an extra 2.5cm (1in) on both the width and the length. Stick in place using double-sided tape and neaten the raw ends. From thin card, cut a circle the same size as the lid. Stick on a circle of wadding to give a padded effect, then cover with fur fabric.

6 Cut a strip of fabric slightly larger than the height of the box and 5cm (2in) longer than its circumference. Fold it in half and sew the short ends together to form a circle. Neaten the two long edges, then stitch six equal compartments. Finally, stick into the box with double-sided tape.

Aromatherapy

For centuries, the pure essences of aromatic plants have been valued for their luxurious scents and their many life-enhancing properties, and your pet will naturally enjoy indulging in the same kind of sybaritic scentsual experience as you do.

Appropriately, it was the Egyptians – worshippers of the noble cat – who take credit for recognizing the full physical and spiritual properties of aromatic essences, and who developed the art from ritual and ceremonial use to massage and personal pleasure.

Your cat will enjoy the beneficial effects of aromatherapy in many ways. Herbal tea bags, if not used for infusions as such, are often appreciated as scented toys in their own right. Fresh growing herbs, or their dried versions, can be brushed against, nibbled at, or played with. And of course your cat will no doubt appreciate, with you, the more subtle effects of aromatic room burners and scents. A lingering fragrance will soon clear the air and promote pleasant thoughts for both cat and owner.

Your cat will be intrigued and fascinated by the range of smells emanating from your aromatherapy kit. (Keep all bottles tightly sealed – essential oils must never be taken internally.)

A dog-shaped toy is tantalizingly stuffed with scented catnip – guaranteed to send your friend into a heightened state one way or the other.

Important Note: Herbs and spices, used fresh, should not harm your cat at all. If you want to try them in essential oil form, perhaps as room burners, then remember that they are very powerful and use only in highly diluted form and follow the labels precisely; don't allow your cat to drink them, and don't use them with pregnant cats. Essential oils can be wonderful natural therapies and remedies, but are never a substitute for proper veterinary advice if your cat is ill – the list opposite is intended as a light-hearted guide.

Basil A herb for depression and the more nervous cat.

Bay A possible remedy for sleeplessness (not usually a cat-related problem, of course).

Camomile An ideal sedative, again not always necessary with snooze-prone pets.

Cinnamon A useful pick-me-up and general tonic, for sluggish cats.

Eucalyptus Good as a head-clearer, perhaps after a heavy night on the tiles.

Frankincense Encourages a more meditative state, perhaps appropriate for the more fractious tom-cat.

Jasmine A luxurious flower that will lift the spirits.

Lavender A pleasant tranquillizing scent that is popular with cats – bunches of fresh and dried lavender will cause much interest.

Marjoram Another herb that will calm and soothe.

Myrrh Usually used for indigestion, perhaps after a day of over-indulgence.

Peppermint A very popular herb with cats (used peppermint herbal tea bags provide hours of fun).

Pine Good, of course, for breathing difficulties and chills.

Rosemary A good pepping-up herb that will aid concentration.

That cats experience mood-enhancement from different aromas is not in question – their sense of smell is much more highly developed than that of humans.

The aromatic herb par excellence is of course the irresistible catnip plant.

Massage

Massage for cats and kittens is an extension of "finger grooming" – and this gentle all-over body rub is the best place to start any massage session. Once your efforts have built up a steady, appreciative purr – you'll be surprised how loud the noise can get – move on to gently caress the rest of your cat's body.

Every once in a while you might think of using some of your own perfumes to give your cat a special treat. *Be very careful though* as highly perfumed toiletries can irritate cats.

A firm back stroke followed by a quick flick up to the tail is an irresistible massage technique that will delight every cat.

The cat prepared for massage . . . creating the right ambience is all-important, as for humans, so have soft towels and the right props to hand.

Massage Sequence

Massage is something that is enjoyed instinctively by cats – one always has the impression that they know a lot more about it than you do.

1 Caress your cat gently behind the ears, either both at the same time or one after the other.

5 Failing this, your cat may enjoy it if, with her facing away from you, you massage her flanks with your fingertips.

2 Now shift your attention to her chest, reaching round in front with both hands to press the centre of the chest, moving the pressure outwards, then circling back to the centre to start again.

6 And back to the head, which may need a slow rubbing with the knuckles.

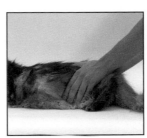

3 Next come the sides, which you can knead more firmly, using both your fingertips and the heels of your hands, running the pressure in a general direction from the neck towards the tail.

The final stage of a successful massage – complete relaxation from whisker to tail tip.

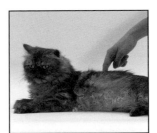

4 A good kneading of the shoulders is often appreciated, and you can try running your thumbs gently down the length of your cat's spine, again from neck to tail. Most cats cannot abide having their tummies rubbed; but a few adore it, and will roll ecstatically over on their backs to make your task easier – rubbing with the front of the knuckles in a rotary motion is best.

Sports, Games and Puss-times

The best sport of all, of course, enjoyed by the cat is that of sleeping, in all its myriad forms – dozing, resting, snoozing and stretching. A full guide to all the techniques involved in these important exercises is provided in this vital chapter. However, when they aren't pursuing the above, there are occasions when your cat will choose to

exert himself in more active pursuits, such as chasing, scratching, and watching and catching things.

All cats secretly remain kittens at heart, and dearly love to play. And of course as well as giving pleasure, frequent games will have therapeutic effects for your pet, providing stimulation and exercise, and keeping them bright-eyed and sharp-clawed.

All work and no play makes for a dull
companion. Every cat needs to be
stretched both physically and
intellectually to fulfil itself – and there is
no better way than through toys, games
and sports. For a complete cat, always
provide lots of stimulation – good food
and a warm bed are only half the job.

Toys of all sorts assist cats to acquire and
enjoy new skills, and to learn about the
world and their role in it. Here, a
playmate stuffed with catnip convinces
this young cat that perhaps dogs aren't so
bad after all!

Snoozing

For cats, there is an art to snoozing which we humans will never fully understand. The feline snooze *artiste* displays a range of positions and perfectly executed techniques which have evolved over the years – and even the least proficient of cats can far surpass anything a human has ever attempted.

Just a few of the basics are outlined below: your cat will demonstrate many personal variations on these principle "asanas" as well as countless thousands of other positions which we have no room to examine here.

Sprawled on Side, One Rear Leg Raised

Most commonly occurs when your cat realizes the time is right for an impromptu snooze midway through a bout of self-grooming. This advanced technique, combining a certain decadence with an undercurrent of humour, is dearly loved by connoisseurs of the genre.

Shelf Posture, with Tail and One Foreleg Dangling

As the name suggests, this is best done on a shelf containing highly fragile and irreplaceable ornaments, although many cats will also produce graceful extemporizations using the back of an expensively upholstered chair. Often the tail can be twitched to and fro to show that snoozing is not just a static artform but one more closely allied to ballet or t'ai chi.

The Doormat

A room bathed in sunlight or the carpet in front of a roaring log fire is a suitable location for this whole-hearted posture. The skill is to make it look as if the body has been transformed into a flattened and lifeless bed of fur.

Don't worry! Out of necessity their physiology has evolved over thousands of years to allow sleep to occur naturally in every conceivable contortion.

Going . . . *To create the mood for snoozing, start by rubbing your finger seductively behind the ear . . .* **going**. . . *Slide round behind the head and nuzzle gently with the palm . . .* **gone** . . . *and leave her dreaming contentedly.*

A nice variation, with the right foreleg neatly tucked under the chin. This cat (above) scored triple ZZZ in the Nap Olympics, snoring away with a gold medal for technical merit and stylistic excellence.

In training, and dreaming of emulating the legendary slumbers of its ancestors, this cat (below) shows complete disregard for the rules of grace, style and form, but scores high on appeal.

Soma Vulgaris (above) – known in the trade as "self-nesting". This is the common or garden "Furball" style, whi all cats will fall back on for everyday use.

In another category, Assisted Snooze, this moggie (right) cuddles up to her favourite scarf for cosy comfort.

Toys and Games

Toys can be improvized from all sorts of objects around the house, and you can have tremendous extended game sessions using something as simple as a spoon. However, probably because of the intensity with which they enjoy their play, cats can very soon tire of a particular toy, so you will need a constantly changing list of fabulous playthings on demand. The best idea if you want to keep your cat contented is to surround her with lots of entrancing toys, both simple and complicated, both incidental and specially made.

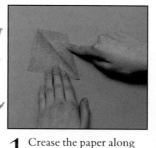

All cats have predatory instincts. If no natural prey animals are in evidence, then hunting-toys like these stuffed mice are a wonderful and socially acceptable substitute. The colours don't matter: this one is in rainbow colours so you can spot it easily when it has rolled behind the back of the bookshelf.

You could make these mice even more tantalizing by making them into a mouse mobile.

Paper Mice

Paper mice won't last for ever, but they're easy to make, decorative, and offer variety and novelty.

You will need:

10cm (4in) square of paper • craft knife • pencil

1 Crease the paper along its diagonal, then open the paper out again. Bring in the side to make a kite shape, creating a sharp corner at the bottom.

Frequently the toy you intended the cat to regard as mock-prey becomes instead an item with the approximate status of "friend".

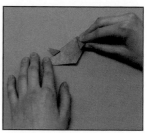

2 Fold the kite shape in half. With a craft knife, cut a V-shaped slit to create the ears. Fold each "V" shape upwards.

3 To create the tail, fold the paper forward, about half the way along, then fold it back on itself again. Draw in the eyes and curl the tail.

Goldfish-bowl Ball

Make sure you choose washable non-shrink, colourfast fabrics – test-wash first if you're unsure.

You will need:

tracing paper • soft pencil • thin card • scissors • 30cm (⅓yd) of 90cm (1yd) wide strong, blue fabric • 25 × 20cm (10 × 8in) yellow fabric, backed with fusible inter-facing • 10 × 10cm (4 × 4in) paler blue fabric • scrap of green fabric • pins • needle and matching thread • scraps of interfacing • strong button thread • 4 gold beads • 4 flat circular plastic squeakers • toy filling • piping cord • blue bias binding

1 Transfer the pattern on page 93 onto thin card. Cut out the pattern pieces: six main pieces in blue, four fish shapes in yellow, a pale blue circle for the top of the bowl, and green leaves.

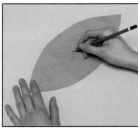

2 Draw a stem onto one of the blue segments. Pin and tack the leaves into position along the stem. Pin a scrap of interfacing behind the blue fabric. Using a machine satin stitch, appliqué the leaf and stitch the wavy stem.

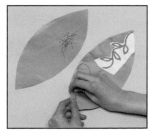

3 Join the appliquéd segment to two other blue segments, and sew the other three blue segments to each other, along the stitching lines, making two half balls. Trim the seams. Don't join the two halves together at this stage.

Your cat can while away hours with a simple toy – so imagine how much fun this ball with squeakers inside will provide.

4 Using strong button thread, sew the fishes' eyes into position. Pin then tack two fish onto each half of the ball, enclosing a squeaker as you do so. Satin stitch around each fish.

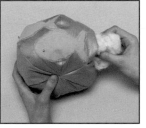

5 Join the two halves of the ball together. Trim the seam. Join the top and bottom of the last seam, leaving a gap. Stuff the ball firmly with toy filling. Slip stitch the opening securely.

6 Enclose the piping cord in the bias binding, and pin onto the pale blue fabric circle. Stitch into position. Turn the circle over, and, enclosing the raw edges, slip stitch it to the top of the ball.

Rugged Pursuits

The outside world holds all kinds of delicious fascinations – whether it be a garden teeming with wildlife; a back alley; an open field or a fish-pond. If your cat is confined in the city then you can easily bring the great outdoors indoors by making toys and games which are evocative of the world outside.

The fact that someone put this entrancing object in the garden for birds, not kittens, is of no relevance whatsoever. They believe it has been erected solely to amuse them.

To make these robins even more tasty, you can fill them with catnip instead of toy filling.

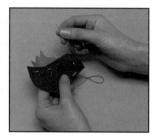

Felt Robins

The purrfect way to introduce your cat to their favourite outdoor pursuit – chasing birds.

1 Trace the pattern pieces from the template on page 92 onto thin card, then cut them out of felt. For each bird you will need two body pieces in red felt, two wings in green felt, one gusset in red felt, a beak in yellow felt and eyes in black felt.

3 Sew the two body pieces together, along the top seam, right sides together. Then sew the gusset in place, leaving a gap for filling. Turn right side out.

You will need:

tracing paper • soft pencil • thin card • scissors • felt: red, green, yellow and black • needle and matching thread • toy filling or fabric wadding

2 Stitch one wing to each body piece along the centre back seam.

4 Stuff firmly with toy filling or scraps of fabric wadding. Slip stitch the gap securely. Sew a beak in position and glue on felt for the eyes.

Tree Scratching Post

The ultimate indoor gym equipment, this de luxe tree-style scratching post will save your furniture all sorts of punishment.

You will need:

cat scratcher • tape measure • green cotton fabric • wadding • lining material • scissors • pins • needle and matching threads • staple gun

For further embellishment, why not add the robins to the tree too?

1 Measure all round one of the platforms on the cat scratcher and cut a rectangle of green material, wadding and lining as long as this and approximately 15cm (6in) wide, adding seam allowances.

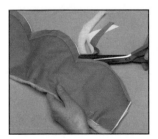

3 Machine along the curved edge, then cut into the corners and snip the curves. Trim the seams.

2 Cut out curved tree shapes on one of the long sides. Then pin the three layers together.

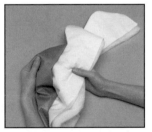

4 Turn to the right side and press flat. Top stitch along the curved seam, 6mm (¼in) from the edge. Fold the seams over on the top edge and machine along the seam. Staple around the platform. Make a "tree" edge for each platform. You can always cover the top in material too.

Games to Play

Anyone who knits will know how much fun a cat can derive from something as simple as a ball of wool. Other common household items can be used as the basis for all sorts of games. Here are a few.

Elastic

Feathers

Corks

String

Pom poms

A ball of string or wool can provide hours of fun. Do keep an eye on things just in case your cat gets into trouble – don't leave her unattended with the toy.

Cotton-reel Racing

You need an empty cotton reel and a relatively uncluttered room. Kneeling at one end of the room, attract your cat's attention and roll the reel rapidly across the carpet towards the opposite wall: it'll naturally tend to veer and swerve. She will race after the reel and pounce on it either before it hits the wall or after it bounces off. If you are feeling competitive, score a point for yourself if the reel hits the wall before she catches it, or a point for her if she snatches the reel triumphantly before it gets there. Your cat will end the game at the appropriate moment by getting bored and walking away; traditionally this is the time to add up the scores and announce the winner. Award the winner a red rosette.

The best playmate your cat can have (besides you, of course) is another cat, even if they do chew an ear off once in a while. If your cat is of normally stable and equitable temperament do make sure she comes into contact with other cats as regularly as possible.

Pawball

Mark a pair of goalposts on the wall or, even better, build a goal from cardboard or use an empty cardboard box. Your cat goes in front of the goal, as keeper. Roll a small rubber ball – not too fast at first – towards her. Once you've both agreed the game of Pawball has properly started, which may take some time, every goal you score counts as a point in your favour; every time your opponent catches the ball before it goes into the goal is a point against you.

Elastic Jumping

Tie something weighty to the end of a length of elastic, or thread a wooden ball onto a piece of wire. Bounce the weight just in front of your cat's nose.

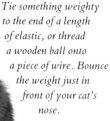

Do this fairly gently at first so that she can catch the "prey", then start to increase the speed and height above her. Once she is engaged and the game is properly under way, start for real.

Score by awarding her a point each time the weight is caught, and yourself a point for every bounce on the elastic before that happens; at the end of the session, divide your own number of points by ten.

Chasing Shadows

Arrange the lighting so that you can cast shadows on the wall using your hands: make butterflies, fish, swans, rabbits, mice and a hundred other shapes – if you feel really inspired, make shadow puppets of favourite shapes from pieces of cardboard and bits of string. Once your cat's attention has been attracted, you can spend half an evening quietly by yourselves while your companion leaps enthusiastically, trying to catch the enticing creatures.

Cats are adept at yoga and were using it for relaxation and deep meditation millions of years before human beings ever thought of it. So rather than teaching your companion, you'll be better off watching her and copying the poses you see her perform.

Your Cat and the Stars

As your cat curls in the basket or languorously stretches out in front of the fire, the stars may seem a very long way away – but of course they directly influence her life as much as they do your own. Cat astrology has not yet become a refined science – there are still too many imponderables, notably the difficulty of ascertaining

a cat's precise time of birth – but you can make a start in understanding your companion's inscrutable character.

The observations in this chapter will enable you to fully please your pet – from selecting favourite foodstuffs and compatible colours, to understanding subtle mood swings and behaviour more sensitively, however erratic and idiosyncratic they might appear to the untrained eye.

As human astrology is increasingly validated by overwhelming scientific and statistical supporting evidence, so cat astrology is only half a whisker behind. There is no doubt that cat characteristics are eerily predictable by star-sign – look up your companion's horoscope here and see for yourself!

Mystic Mog in characteristic pose doing a horoscope.

Aries
21 March–19 April

Aries cats are pushers: they are ever-ready to try something new as soon as it occurs to them. Unfortunately, they tend to have little staying power, so very often their ambitious plans come to nothing. They can be tremendous fun to be with, although you have to be prepared to be very tolerant – life with an Aries cat can be extremely rumbustious, so be prepared to say farewell to delicate ornaments and furnishings. Their independent streak can be a nuisance at times, but Aries cats compensate you for this with their unbounded affection.

Aries cats are daring and outgoing and likely to be explorers

Give your Aries kitten their own house to destroy before they destroy yours

Red is the colour and football is the game

If you don't have a dustbin in the alley, give your Aries cat your leftovers instead

★ *Compatible cats*: Leo; Sagittarius
★ *Compatible owners*: same as cats
★ *Favourite colour*: red
★ *Lucky number*: 9

★ *Favourite food*: fish of all types – particularly fish from dustbins
★ *Greatest dislike*: being kept for long periods in an enclosed space

★ *Other cat who may share this starsign*: Orlando the Marmalade Cat
★ *Attributes*: enthusiasm; independence; devotion; fecklessness

Taurus
20 April–20 May

Taurus cats tend to be slow-moving and to take a while making up their minds about something: once it's been made up, however, you may find it next to impossible to deter them. A Taurus cat will give you unswerving loyalty and friendship, but do beware of one thing: Taurus cats are slow to anger, and this may give you the illusion that they never lose their tempers. They do, and the eventual outburst can be very vigorous indeed. So be sensitive and considerate to your Taurus cat, and make sure you are consistently harmonious and concessionary.

Give your Taurean cat a wendy house all of its own so that it always has somewhere that it can call home

Sardines for supper

Taurus cats will give you unswerving loyalty and friendship

Pastel-coloured pussy boots for trips to town

★ *Compatible cats*: Gemini, although be prepared for fights; Libra
★ *Compatible owners*: Taurus
★ *Favourite colour*: pastel shades
★ *Lucky number*: 11

★ *Favourite food*: sardines
★ *Greatest dislike*: instability of any kind, such as frequent house moves – although fidelity to its owner enables it to cope

★ *Other cat who may share this starsign*: Dinah (from *Through the Looking-Glass*)
★ *Attributes*: loyalty; good-nature; temper

Gemini

21 May–21 June

Gemini cats are usually frisky individuals, and among the most entertaining of all felines. Their frequent, unpredictable mood changes can be unsettling but, once you are used to them, are a constant source of pleasure. Gemini cats are insatiably curious, and will pry into everything. Be sensitive to your Gemini cat's moods: just because she seems full of *joie de vivre*, don't assume she is unfailingly happy.

Geminis are full of whims and fancies so it is impossible to predict what foods they will want. You may make a mistake!

Gemini cats are nosey so keep titbits and treats out of sight

Gemini cats have little patience and they are likely to throw their feet in the air at the slightest obstacle

Yellow and gold are a Gemini cat's favourite colours

★ *Compatible cats*: Taurus
★ *Compatible owners*: Capricorn
★ *Favourite colour*: yellow and gold
★ *Lucky number*: 3

★ *Favourite food*: Gemini cats are notorious for going off foods, so have several choices to hand
★ *Greatest dislike*: boredom

★ *Other cat who may share this starsign*: Thomas O'Malley (*The Aristocats*)
★ *Attributes*: curiosity; energy; bounciness; indecisiveness

Cancer

22 June–22 July

Cancer cats tend to be sensitive creatures and devoted pets so long as you are as attuned to their moods as they are to yours. A Cancer cat will have a strongly developed sense of what is fair and what is not, so be prepared for some early "discussions" as you establish whose territory is whose. Cancer cats can be very good "watchcats": they become extremely territorial, and will see off other animals, including dogs much larger than themselves.

Being sensitive souls, Cancer cats do not like to be upset

Cancer cats can be very good "watchcats"

Ring the changes for the daring Cancerian with a fruit cocktail

Even the smallest Cancer kitten will have a go at a dog if it is invading its space

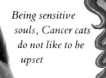

★ *Compatible cats*: Scorpio
★ *Compatible owners*: Scorpio and Aquarius
★ *Favourite colour*: earth tones

★ *Lucky number*: any number but 13
★ *Favourite food*: interesting food of different textures
★ *Greatest dislike*: emotional upset

★ *Other cat who may share this starsign*: Old Possum
★ *Attributes*: moral rectitude; sensitivity; possessiveness

Leo

23 July–22 August

The lion is the king of cats, and most Leo cats assume themselves to be wild and regal. If you bring a Leo cat into your home, expect it to be in no doubt as to who is going to be in charge. Initially they can seem haughty and unapproachable, but once you have earned the friendship of a Leo cat, you will have a friend for life. Leos can be difficult with other cats who are not prepared to be pack-followers; they will regard it as their right that their food is served first and that their helping is significantly larger. So be prepared for some initial upsets if introducing a Leo cat to others.

Leo cats often behave and even look like lions

Puppies have an annoying habit of being disrespectful, which rubs Leo cats up the wrong way

An imperial purple feather boa for an imperial cat

Leos like the very best things in life, such as fresh salmon

★ *Compatible cats*: Aries, Leo or Sagittarius
★ *Compatible owners*: Aries, Taurus or Leo – someone with a strong character

★ *Favourite colour*: imperial purple
★ *Lucky number*: 1
★ *Favourite food*: salmon
★ *Greatest dislike*: puppies

★ *Other cat who may share this starsign*: Shere Khan (from *The Jungle Book*)
★ *Attributes*: entertaining; self-centred; theatrical; responsible

Virgo

23 August–22 September

Virgo cats tend to be quiet, self-effacing, neat and exact, and may seem to be remarkably cool to your approaches. Don't be misled into thinking that this is a sign of arrogance – far from it, because Virgo cats, while often highly intelligent, tend habitually to underestimate their own worth and be consequently shy and unable to believe that you are so devoted to them.

Full of confidence in her favourite green coat

Once Virgo cats are convinced you love them, they will return your adoration in full measure

Virgo cats hate any form of emotional insecurity so treat them with care and respect

Bland creamed cod's roe jazzed up in a fishy mould

★ *Compatible cats*: Capricorn
★ *Compatible owners*: any sign
★ *Favourite colour*: green
★ *Lucky number*: 7, though 6 will do

★ *Favourite food*: a general inclination towards blandness might suggest creamed cod roe
★ *Greatest dislike*: not being loved

★ *Other cat who may share this starsign*: Cat Ballou
★ *Attributes*: sensitive; self-obsessed; reserved; smart

Libra

23 September–23 October

Libra cats can be sociable and charming, and normally can be persuaded to see things your way. They generally take a long time to weigh things up but, as with Taurus cats, once they have come to a decision it can be next to impossible to divert them from it. They generally get on well with people and with other cats, and are usually prepared, after the necessary period of decision-making, to join in wholeheartedly with whatever the rest of the gang has determined to do. Once a Libra cat has decided to trust you, do be aware that you must be worthy of that trust: any betrayal would be cruel.

Libra cats do not like big dogs, possibly because their emotional equilibrium is upset

Although pink is a Libran's favourite colour, pale green and blue are also popular choices

Libra cats dislike living alone, and need a happy and lasting relationship

Mackerel for dinner

★ *Compatible cats*: Taurus, Aquarius, Pisces
★ *Compatible owners*: no special preferences, although Libra cats do get on particularly well with Sagittarians

★ *Favourite colour*: pink
★ *Lucky number*: 19
★ *Favourite food*: mackerel, probably because of the scales
★ *Greatest dislike*: large dogs; ghosts

★ *Other cat who may share this starsign*: Top Cat
★ *Attributes*: arrogance; sociability; sulkiness; determination; indecisiveness; idealism

Scorpio
24 October–21 November

Of all cats, Scorpios are likely to be the most promiscuous – in every sense of the word – they are the animals for whom the term "alley cat" could have been invented. They also tend to be the most psychologically complicated and interesting of all cats, although their natural egocentricity can be tiring at times. They give you the outward manifestations of affection easily enough – they will make up to anyone, if they think it is in their interests to do so – but earning their deeper love can require great patience on your part. Once you have done so, however, you could hope for no better companion.

Watch out for the egocentricity of Scorpio cats – they like to be in the limelight

Scorpio cats are little devils

Make your Scorpio cat a maroon cushion for her to sit on during her moody moments

If you are on a tight budget but want to treat your Scorpio cat, settle for a plate of tomatoes

★ *Compatible cats*: Cancer
★ *Compatible owners*: another Scorpio can be the best bet – if you're a bit of an alley cat yourself, then this might be your ideal pet!

★ *Favourite colour*: deep red or maroon
★ *Lucky number*: 111
★ *Favourite food*: caviare and tomatoes
★ *Greatest dislike*: being kept in

★ *Other cat who may share this starsign*: Fritz the Cat
★ *Attributes*: sensitivity; spirituality; intense loyalty; temper and moodiness

Sagittarius

22 November–21 December

Although their characters can sometimes be flawed by over-eagerness – they have a tendency to act first and think afterwards – Sagittarian cats can be the finest pets of all. They have a certain honesty that is unusual in felines, and they are generally prepared to demonstrate their affection for you in a boisterous, good-humoured fashion. Sagittarius is quite a strong sign, so the Sagittarian cat usually gets on well with others and also, notably, with dogs.

Purchase a double bowl so that you can give your Sagittarian cat a choice of foods at the same sitting

Sagittarian cats have a tendency to like dark colours mixed together, so tartans are an ideal fabric for them

Oddly enough Sagittarian cats get on well with dogs

Sagittarians make enthusiastic and good-natured pets

★ *Compatible cats*: Aries or Leo
★ *Compatible owners*: Aries or Leo
★ *Favourite colour*: dark colours
★ *Lucky number*: 22

★ *Favourite food*: Sagittarian cats like a constantly varied and always interesting diet
★ *Greatest dislike*: bureaucats

★ *Other cat who may share this starsign*: Tom (of *Tom & Jerry*)
★ *Attributes*: enthusiasm; dynamism; good-nature; simplicity

Capricorn
22 December–19 January

Like their human counterparts, Capricorn cats usually have the habit of confronting life's obstacles head-on, tending to charge through them rather than trying to devise ways of avoiding them. This can be both a strength and a weakness. Despite this gung-ho attitude, they often remain calm in difficult situations, and this has given them the reputation of being callous, calculating cats. Do not be deceived! A heart of gold lurks within.

Capricorn cats are addicts of grooming and being dolled up

If you give your cat chicken, make sure that you remove all the bones

Capricorn cats are often superficially reserved

Capricorn cats have a particular penchant for black chic

★ *Compatible cats*: Virgo
★ *Compatible owners*: Sagittarius
★ *Favourite colour*: black and brown
★ *Lucky number*: 12

★ *Favourite food*: fish and poultry, although very adaptable – often like vegetables more than most cats
★ *Greatest dislike*: locked fridges

★ *Other cat who may share this starsign*: Pussy Galore (from *Goldfinger*)
★ *Attributes*: intriguing; courageous; devoted; reliable

Aquarius

20 January–18 February

Like Scorpio cats, Aquarian cats can be psychologically complex, but they lack the broody, dark aspect of the Scorpio cat; this may render them less interesting, but it also makes them a lot easier to live with. Gregarious by nature, they can nevertheless reject all their current companions once they are convinced they are unlikely to get their own way today. Many Aquarian cats have artistic aspirations; though they can be creative without following through on their ideas. Aquarian cats also have a highly spiritual element to their psychological make-up – they revel in the New Age.

Allow your Aquarian cat to fully explore its mystical side by buying her a crystal ball

Lightly poached cod is a favourite

Aquarian cats love anything that is a deep shade of blue

Being creative and artistic, Aquarian cats are likely to be untidy

★ *Compatible cats*: Libra, Pisces
★ *Compatible owners*: Capricorn, Pisces
★ *Favourite colour*: electric blue

★ *Lucky number*: 8
★ *Favourite food*: poached cod
★ *Greatest dislike*: having to pay attention to detail

★ *Other cat who may share this starsign*: Irena Dubrovna (from *Cat People*)
★ *Attributes*: artistic; mystical; open; individualistic; unpredictable

Pisces

19 February–20 March

Pisces cats are the hippies of the feline world. Friendly and sympathetic, often quite shy, they have good intentions but are generally too lacking in concentration to put them into practice. They tend to bumble along from day to day, never quite getting their act together but always somehow emerging from every difficulty unscathed. They are exceptionally affectionate – probably too much so for their own good.

Any exotic fish will go down well – shark, swordfish or squid

Piscean cats are ideal for fun and games

Piscean cats tend to be very emotional

A fishy ornament for a fishy cat

★ *Compatible cats*: Aquarius, Libra
★ *Compatible owners*: no preferences
★ *Favourite colour*: sea-green
★ *Lucky number*: 2

★ *Favourite food*: fish – of course! – with a preference for the exotic
★ *Greatest dislike*: Pisces cats seem to have no particular detestations

★ *Other cat who may share this starsign*: The Cheshire Cat
★ *Attributes*: indecisive; genuine; good-spirited; reserved; vague

Cat Perks

However much we love our companions, we have to acknowledge that their contemporary lifestyle is not entirely natural to them. Good owners are constantly aware of this, and always try to provide those little extras that make their deserving companions feel comfortable and special. Celebrations come infrequently during the year, so think of inventing a few new ones and have a regular routine of treats and pampering sessions as special gifts for deserving kitties. In this section you'll find suggestions and inspirations for hundreds of tiny touches that make all the difference.

For celebrations, special days and just for fun, pamper your pal with luxuries and the things she loves. If it's the thought that counts, there are inspirations here for a hundred sensitive gestures and sensational surprises.

Using very simple craft skills – all explained and shown in this chapter – you can make hundreds of treats and spectacular gifts for your companion, and personalize them in dozens of different ways.

Gifts

Every day should be a special day in your cat's life, so there's no need to wait for Christmas or a birthday. Presents can be practical – a new bowl, for example – or joyously frivolous. The most important thing is that they are given and received with love . . .

Birthday Album

A book to chart your cat's family tree, to hold photographs, and for noting down favourite recipes and important events and dates.

You will need:

hardback notebook • patterned paper • pencil • scissors • PVA glue • cartridge paper • paper doilies • gold spray paint • craft knife • pictures of cats and flowers • ribbon

Whether sucked . . .

nibbled . . .

1 Place the book on the wrong side of the patterned paper. Draw a margin of about 4cm (1½in) around it. Cut the paper to this size. Cut off the corners to create mitred joins then stick the paper to the cover.

2 Cut two pieces of cartridge paper to fit inside the front and back of the cover, leaving a small margin down the inside. Stick the paper in position. To decorate the cover, spray paper doilies with gold paint and cut them into pretty shapes. Also cut out flowers and pictures of cats from postcards, photographs and wrapping paper. Glue a ribbon onto the cover allowing enough at each end to tie a bow. Then add the decoration to the book.

. . . or chewed, every gift from you to your companion will provide the kinds of spiritual sustenance, moral nourishment and physical pleasure that feed the inner cat.

A purrrrsonal record of your cat's life.

Cat-o-Fish Tails

Make a puppet out of card for your cat, and the two of you can have hours of fascination watching it twitch and jerk. The basic design could be adapted to make rabbits, mice, fish or other cats.

You will need:

cartridge paper • soft pencil • craft knife • acrylic paints: purple, green, blue, red and black • paintbrush • ribbon • PVA glue • coloured string

1 Draw all the pieces of the puppet onto cartridge paper – two legs, a torso, two arms, a cat's face and a collar. Cut out all of the shapes then paint all the pieces, detailing the design. Glue the head and collar onto the torso.

2 When dry, glue a piece of ribbon onto the front of the torso to make a cummerbund. Glue another piece to the back of the face to make a hat.

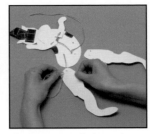

3 Pierce two holes at the top of each limb and four holes in the torso onto which each limb will be attached. Tie a knot in a piece of string and thread it through from the front of the torso through each arm and back through the other hole in the torso. Tie off in a knot at the front. Make sure the arms are loose enough to move up and down. Take another piece of string and repeat for the legs.

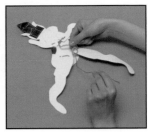

4 Take a piece of string and tie it to make the connecting string between the arms and legs. Leave a length as the draw-string.

5 Then cut a goldfish shape out of card, paint it and tie it to the end of the middle string.

Hang this magnif-i-cat mobile within your cat's reach and watch her go wild – as she pulls the tail the limbs fly up . . . be prepared to make another one shortly.

The Sacred Image

Your cat is central to your life, so celebrate her importance – and flatter her – by glorifying her image in tributes both serious and amusing. Needlecrafts, collage, painting, framing . . . the methods are many, and the results will provide beautiful objects and wonderful reminders of your companion through the stages of her life.

Immortalize your cat by making a wall plaque of her portrait.

Cross-stitch Sampler

Samplers make distinctive adornments for any home, so embroider one specially to hang above the cat basket, to show how much you care.

1 Draw your design onto graph paper using coloured pencils or pens.

Capture those early days in a cross-stitch sampler.

You will need:

graph paper 10 squares to 1in (2.5cm) • coloured pencils or pens • 11-count cross-stitch fabric in cream • embroidery hoop • tacking thread in contrasting colour • sewing needle • tapestry needle, size 26 • stranded cotton in a variety of colours • scissors

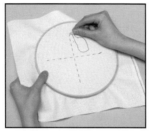

2 Place the fabric in an embroidery hoop. Mark the centre of the canvas with coloured thread, as shown.

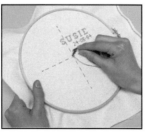

3 Work the sampler in cross–stitch using the method shown on page 95. Remember that the top diagonal stitches of each cross should always slant in the same direction.

Pop-art Portrait

The ultimate gift for contemporary cats, an Andy Warhol-inspired portrait of your special pet.

You will need:

photograph of your cat • paper correction fluid • four sheets of different coloured paper • scissors • pencil • glue • red acrylic paint • tissue or paintbrush • four sheets of coloured paper approximately 30 × 24cm (12 × 9½in) • white card

1 Choose a favourite photograph of your cat, ideally one which has good contrast, and whiten out the area around the face. Make some bold white marks to delineate ears and eyebrows.

Sexier than Marilyn and more irresistible than a can of soup, your cat makes the perfect model for a $4.5m-style portrait that costs only pennies to reinterpret.

2 Photocopy the image onto coloured paper, enlarging it to cover an area 15 × 15cm (6 × 6in). Make four copies, all on different coloured pieces of paper. Cut out the faces.

3 Trace outlines of parts of the faces onto the leftover scraps of paper and cut out. Stick the coloured highlights onto faces of a contrasting colour.

4 Dab paint lightly onto a couple of the faces with a tissue or a paintbrush.

5 Glue the four cat faces onto the four sheets of coloured paper. Mount these onto the white card.

Christmas Cat

Roast turkey with stuffing, presents around the tree, a stocking full of surprises . . . there's a lot to interest your cat around Christmas time. A festive meal with all the trimmings, designed exclusively around your cat's favourite foods, is just the start. Think of making a special cracker or two out of rice paper, with savoury treats inside. Or make an Advent calendar, with special titbits behind each "window". Or go to town and fill a stocking full of delectable treats. All in all, there are hundreds of ways you can make Christmas a memorable time not just for your cat but also for yourself.

Christmas card cats in the perfect festive tableaux.

Queen of the Nile Gift Wrap

Bastet was the Egyptian goddess who appeared as a cat. All cats were sacred to her, so what could be better as a gift-wrap design?

1 Trace the templates of the cat and symbols on page 93, and draw them onto thin card. Cut them out.

3 Use a gold-leaf effect to highlight certain areas. Place the stencil over a painted area. Dab through the card with glue and place a layer of gold leaf over the glue. When dry, remove the stencil and gently brush and blow away any excess leaf.

You will need:

tracing paper • soft pencil • thin card • craft knife • sheet of textured plain paper • masking tape • stencil brush • acrylic paints: black, terracotta and purple • PVA glue • gold leaf

2 Place the stencil onto the sheet of paper and secure it with masking tape. Using the stencil brush, apply the paint but do not overload the brush with paint. Move the stencil to another part of the paper until you have covered the whole surface.

This cat-festooned paper will provide as much fun to play with as the present inside.

Stocking Fillers

*A tasty
sisal fish*

*An elastic
pom pom*

*A furry
mouse*

*A spider
on elastic*

Christmas Cookies

*Treat your kitty to a real
Christmas feast of these
festive fishy biscuits.*

*225g/8oz plain wholemeal flour
1 × 200g/7oz can pressed
cods roe
50g/2oz vegetable fat
1 egg*

*The perfect
Christmas TV
snack.*

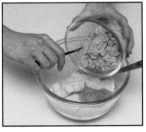

1 Preheat the oven to 180°C/350°F/Gas 4. Put all the ingredients into a mixing bowl.

2 Mix into a soft dough, adding a little water if the mixture is too stiff.

3 Turn out onto a floured surface and roll out to about 0.5cm (¼in) thick.

4 Cut out the biscuits and place on a baking sheet and cook in the oven until crisp and golden. Allow to cool and then store in an airtight tin.

How to Communi-cat

Having taken every necessary measure to ensure your companion's physical well-being, what about the inner cat? Good diet, plenty of exercise, comfortable surroundings, warmth and affection – plus a little work on your own equability – will normally ensure that you have a happy, well-adjusted, secure and fulfilled cat, but you can go further towards ensuring her emotional well-being by learning how to communicate. Here are some tips.

Cats have a million ways of talking amongst themselves, but need encouragement to communicate with you.

Speaking

Cats rarely use sounds to communicate with each other – except when threatening to fight – whereas we use them all the time. Domesticated cats have noticed this and learned to employ distinctive calls when wanting to be fed, let out, welcoming you home or even triumphantly bringing in a new item of prey from the garden to "share" with you. In these circumstances your cat is making a big effort to talk to you, so learn the meanings of these different calls and respond appropriately.

Trusting

Kneel down in front of your cat and, with your hands behind your back or well out of the way, slowly lean forward until your face is just an inch or two from hers, keeping your eyes open. Because you are presenting your vulnerable eyes so close to her you are showing that you're neither aggressive nor frightened – in short, that you're a trusting friend. If she feels like responding in kind, you'll find your nose being gently brushed by her nose or forehead. (Do not under any circumstances try this with a cat whom you do not know well, or with a neurotic, unpredictable cat.)

Eye Contact

Catch her attention and lock gazes. Then, without making a great production of it, blink very slowly, just once, and keep your eyes locked on hers. If she is relaxed and content, the reply will come in the form of a responsive slow blink. It may take a while before she catches on that you're making the effort to communicate in "cat language" (which this is), but gradually you will be able to say "I love you and you love me" whenever you want to.

All cats are wary and defensive at first. But trust, and showing you are not scared to be vulnerable, breaks down aggression and protective display, and eventually results in a gentle response.

Telling the Tale

Different cats can use different tail signals, so study your own cat's individual movements. In general, however:

■ *tail held in a low curve*: confident and content
■ *tail held upright*: alert, confident, possibly aggressive
■ *tail upright and waving*: possibly angry, more likely just keenly interested
■ *tail wrapped around snoozing cat, or gently beating the floor with a slow, regular thud*: completely relaxed and secure
■ *tail between the legs*: insecurity, possibly fear
■ *tail wrapped around the legs*: fear

This tail curved around the legs shows nervousness . . . while the upright wave indicates keen interest.

Held upright, the tail says, "I'm confident, and maybe even a little full of myself today"

Ready to play?

A cat who's busy relaxing may want to carry on snoozing, but if you want a cuddle, approach gently and stroke very lightly, just brushing the tips of the fur. If in the mood for affection, your cat will raise her head and respond with a lick of your hand or face, or may move her head up towards your hand indicating that some more vigorous stroking would be very much appreciated. In the latter case, if the cat stretches out both forelegs to the front, this will be a signal that she is prepared to forsake her nap for more animated play.

If your cat responds to an advance by leaning into your strokes or fondling and nuzzling back, she is graciously indicating that more touching would be acceptable!

The Purrrrfect Day

Days like Christmas will of course be times when you want to pay your cat particular attention, but obviously you won't be able to concentrate your entire focus on your cat – you will have human obligations to fulfil as well. So, every now and then, allocate a day completely to her, designating it a Purrrrfect Day.

All the activities that your companion loves best can be packed into this single day. Presents, gourmet meals, friends to visit, snoozing, playing outside, and a few games as well. For the day, you could endeavour to communicate in "cat" rather than in "human" as much as possible, and set a quiet time aside for a long period of stroking and grooming.

Play soft and mellow melodies to enhance your companion's catnaps.

The complete playtime toy for a kitten . . . it also stops your furniture from being destroyed . . . a present for both of you.

The purrrrfect pampered pussy cat.

A pal to play with is a pal indeed.

Stroking is an integral part of the Purrrrfect Day. Except when your companion wants to snooze, eat or hunt in the garden, make sure you offer a lot of affectionate stroking and tickling – show her she's the most important person in your world!

Cod in Parsley Sauce

The purrrrfect ending to a purrrrfect day.

75g/3oz cod fillet, skinned
85ml/3 fl oz milk
15g/½oz butter
1 tsp flour
1 tsp chopped parsley

Poach the cod in milk until cooked. Remove and allow to cool. Using a whisk, beat the flour and butter into cooking liquor and slowly bring to the boil, stirring until thickened. Add parsley and allow to cool. Pour the sauce onto a plate and add the fish.

A possible end for the Purrrrfect Day: settling down in front of a roaring log fire for snoozing, stroking, and just being together.

Templates

You can either use the templates the
same size as they are reproduced here
or enlarge them. To use the same
size, simply trace them, transfer onto
paper and cut them out. To enlarge,
either use a grid system or a
photocopier. For the grid method,
trace the template and draw a grid of
evenly-spaced squares over your
tracing. To scale up, draw a larger
grid onto another piece of paper.
Copy the outline onto the second
grid by taking each square
individually and drawing the relevant
part of the outline in the larger
square. Finally, draw over the lines
to make sure they are continuous.

Stencilling

Stencils can be cut from thin card or
specialist waxy stencil card. Trace the
pattern onto the card then cut it out
with a craft knife. Secure the stencil
firmly to the surface that is to be
painted. To achieve a good, clean
shape, the paint needs to be thick so
that it does not run and you should
use the paint sparingly. Apply the
paint using a light dabbing
movement. Wait until the paint has
dried before moving the stencil and
painting the next shape.

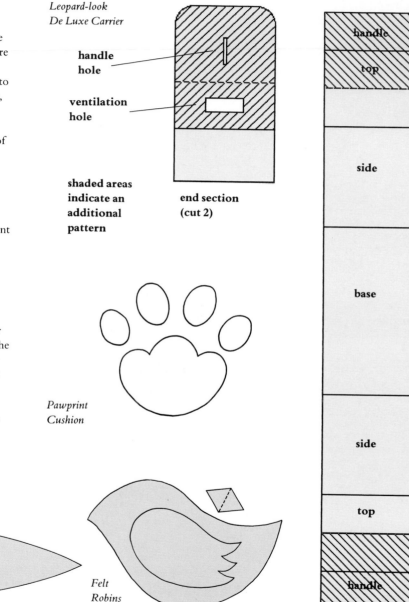

*Leopard-look
De Luxe Carrier*

**handle
hole**

**ventilation
hole**

**shaded areas
indicate an
additional
pattern**

**end section
(cut 2)**

handle

top

side

base

side

top

handle

*Pawprint
Cushion*

*Felt
Robins*

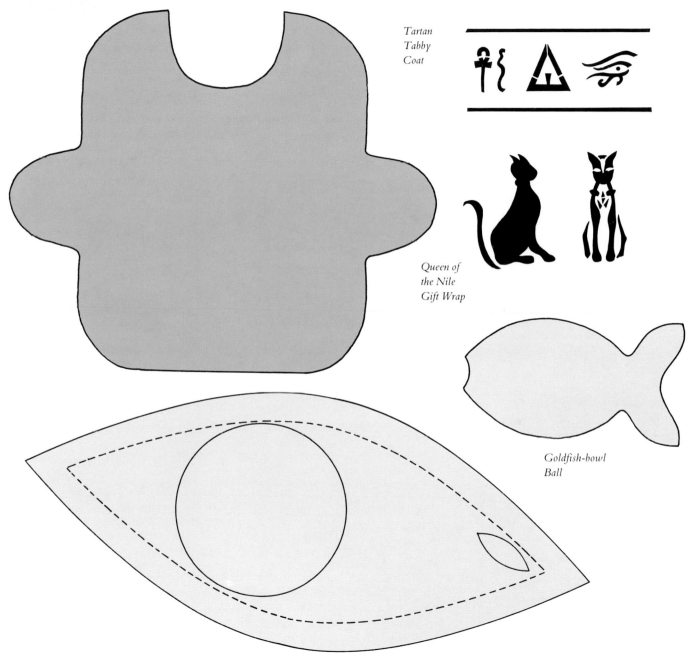

*Tartan
Tabby
Coat*

*Queen of
the Nile
Gift Wrap*

*Goldfish-bowl
Ball*

Basic Sewing Techniques

Tacking

Tacking

This is a temporary stitch used to hold seams together before sewing. The stitches should be between 0.5cm (¼in) and 1cm (⅜in) long.

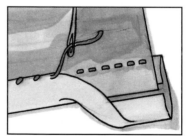
Applying Bias Binding

Applying Bias Binding

Pin the bias binding on the right side of the fabric with right sides facing and raw edges aligning. Tack and machine stitch in position along the raw edges with a 0.5cm (¼in) seam allowance. Remove the tacking stitches, turn the free edge of the binding over to the wrong side of the fabric and turn it under itself to create a clean edge. Slip stitch with matching thread to secure in place.

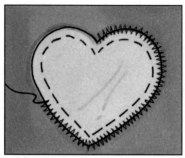
Machine Appliqué

Machine Appliqué

Machine appliqué is quick and hardwearing. Cut out the motif, then pin and tack in position on the main fabric. Set the sewing machine to a close zig zag or satin stitch and sew around the edges of the shape so that the raw edges are covered completely.

Quilting

To achieve good results, the layers of fabric you are working with – usually top fabric, wadding and backing – need to be secured together before you begin to stitch. This will prevent the layers from slipping out of position. To do this, lay the backing fabric wrong side up on a flat, hard surface. Lay the other two layers over the top, ending with the top fabric, right side up. Pin, then tack the layers together. For small pieces you can use safety pins instead.

You can then either machine- or hand-sew the quilt. For quilting by hand, work the design using small, evenly spaced running stitches. If quilting by machine, work a small practice piece. A "walking foot" fitted to your machine will help prevent the fabric layers moving and causing puckering.

Tailor's Tacks

Tailor's Tacks

This is the most accurate way to transfer markings from a paper pattern onto double fabric. With the pattern still pinned in place, make a tiny slit through the paper across the symbol to be marked. Using a double thread, tack several loops through both layers. Remove the pattern, gently ease the fabric apart, and cut the loops. The tufts of thread.

Basic Stitches

Running Stitch

Running stitch is one of the most commonly used stitches. It should be used for hand quilting designs and gathering, keeping the stitches small and evenly spaced on both the front and back of the piece. Work running stitch by passing the needle regularly in and out of the fabric to create the pattern.

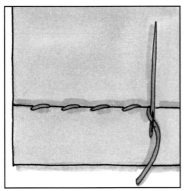

Slip Stitch

Slip Stitch

Slip stitch is used to join together two folded edges. When joining two folds, the stitches are almost invisible and are worked from the right side of the fabric. Pick up a couple of threads of the single fabric and carefully slip the needle through the fold for about 0.5cm (¼in). Draw the thread through to make a tiny stitch.

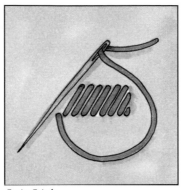

Satin Stitch

Satin Stitch

Satin stitch looks easy but some practice is needed to work it neatly. It is used for filling in and outlining. Ensure the fabric is always held tautly in a frame to prevent puckering. Carry the thread across the area to be filled, then return it back underneath the fabric as near as possible to the point from which the needle emerged.

Stab Stitch

Stab Stitch

Stab stitch is used for attaching things to fabric almost invisibly or for quilting through many layers and it is literally a stabbing movement. Bring the needle up through the layers of fabric, then make a tiny stitch and push the needle through underneath. Make a larger stitch under the fabric and repeat.

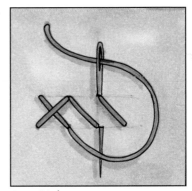

Cross Stitch

Cross Stitch

Cross stitch is the best known of all embroidery stitches; it was used by the ancient Egyptians and more recently for the samplers made by nineteenth-century schoolchildren. It is worked in two parts, and the top stitches should always lie in the same direction. For large areas, work a row of diagonal stitches from right to left, then complete the crosses with a second row of diagonal stitches in the opposite direction.

Index

Acknowledgements

The publisher would like to thank the following for creating items for photography.
Petra Boase: Pussy Place Mat 43. Lucinda Ganderton: Pawprint Cushion 15; Fancy Brush 50; Vanity Case 51. Lesley Grant: Cross-stitch Sampler 84. Carole Hart: Tartan Tabby Coat 22–3; Catmaiden

Collar 26; Jewelled Collar 27. Paul Jackson: Paper Mice 60. Wendy Massey: Bow Tie 29; Goldfish-bowl Ball 61; Felt Robins 62; Tree Scratching Post 63. Thomasina Smith: Sea-cat Box 11; Jungle Carrier 12; Leopard-look De Luxe Carrier 13; Skyscraper Privacy Screen 17; Fish Reflections 19; Mice and Cheese Plates 42; Birthday Album 82; Cat-o-Fish Tails 83; Pop-art Portrait 85; Queen of the Nile Gift Wrap 86.

The publisher would like to thank Sue Hall, Melinda Ellis and Hazel Taylor for their help during the photography sessions, and Georges of Chelsea for their

generosity in loaning items for photography: screen 16; ornaments 18; green coat 22; t-shirt, black coat and harness 25; and additional grooming equipment and toys.

We would also like to thank the following. Canac Pet Products: tartan mat 14. Companions: plaque 84. Cosmo Place Studio: hand-painted china plates. Cover up Designs Ltd: cat bowls and food jars. Emap Pursuit Publishing Ltd: image of the four-poster bed 10. Philip Yeast Products Ltd: wendy house 10. Purves and Purves: cat plates. Something Special Ltd: draught excluder 16.